W9-BVM-555

# SUPER SKILLS

# HOW TO CODE

## IN 10 EASY LESSONS

## SEAN McMANUS

Walter Foster Jr.

Quarto is the authority on a wide range of topics.
Quarto educates, entertains and enriches the lives of our readers—
enthusiasts and lovers of hands-on living.
www.quartoknows.com

© Quarto Publishing Group USA Inc.
Published by Walter Foster Jr.,
an imprint of Quarto Publishing Group USA Inc.
All rights reserved. Walter Foster Jr. is trademarked.

First published in the UK by
Marshall Editions
Part of The Quarto Group
The Old Brewery
6 Blundell Street
London N7 9BH

Publisher: Zeta Jones
Art Director: Susi Martin
Managing Editor: Laura Knowles
Design: Punch Bowl Design
Original Illustrations: Venetia Dean

All rights reserved. No part of this publication may be reproduced,
stored in any retrieval systems, or transmitted in any form or by
any means, electronic, mechanical, photocopying, recording or
otherwise, without the prior permission of the publisher.

**6 Orchard Road, Suite 100**
**Lake Forest, CA 92630**
**quartoknows.com**
**Visit our blogs @quartoknows.com**

Printed in China
3  5  7  9  10  8  6  4

Throughout this book, screenshots show the author's
Scratch coding project examples. Scratch is developed by
the Lifelong Kindergarten Group at the MIT Media Lab.
See http://scratch.mit.edu.

# ABOUT THE AUTHOR

Sean McManus is a Code Club volunteer, helping
to teach programming and web design at a primary
school in London, UK. He is the author of *Scratch
Programming in Easy Steps*, *Web Design in
Easy Steps*, and the co-author of *Raspberry Pi For
Dummies*. Visit his website at **www.sean.co.uk**
for Scratch resources and more.

Hello
World!

# CONTENTS

# WELCOME TO THE WORLD OF CODING

We're surrounded by computers, phones, and tablets giving us a constant flow of information and entertainment. With the right software (or apps), they can do almost anything we want. But the question is: What do you do if you can't find the right software? The answer: Write it yourself.

Coding is all about giving instructions to a digital device, using a language it understands, so that it does exactly what you want it to. In this book, you'll learn how to code your own computer games and design a website where you can tell the world all about them.

## ARE YOU READY?

Yes you are! You don't need any special skills or knowledge to start with. Everybody can learn to code, and the software you need for the projects in this book doesn't cost anything. You will need to use an Internet-connected computer based on Windows, Mac OS, or Linux, but if you don't have one, check whether your school or library can help. If you have a Raspberry Pi, some of the Scratch programs won't work for you, but you can build your website using Leafpad.

## HOW THIS BOOK IS ORGANIZED

This book will introduce you to 10 core skills for coding. We'll be using the programming language Scratch to make a game, but many of the skills you learn here are also useful in other programming languages that you might learn later. It is best to read the chapters in the right order, because each chapter builds on the previous chapter. If you skip a chapter, you might miss something important.

## EXPERIMENT!

As you work through this book, you'll see code examples to try out. Feel free to experiment with the code and see if you can improve it. As you build up your coding skills, you might want to go back to the earlier examples and use your new knowledge to improve the basic programs you've already created.

## IT'S NOT ALL ABOUT GAMES

The examples used in this book are mostly games, but the skills you acquire can be used to make all kinds of software. Games make excellent examples because it is easy to test them and see how they work. It's a lot of fun to make them and to play them! But, if you want to write software that makes music, art, or helps with your homework, you'll be able to do that too. Once you've learned how to code, you can make the computer do whatever you want.

THE EXAMPLES IN THIS BOOK WERE MADE USING SCRATCH 2.0 AND USE MANY OF ITS NEW FEATURES. IF YOU'RE USING AN OLDER VERSION OF SCRATCH, SOME PROJECTS WON'T WORK.

## BEWARE OF THE BUGS

From time to time, your programs probably won't work as you expect them to. There might be an instruction in the wrong place or the wrong number in a box. This is a problem that even professional coders face every day. So don't panic: just check your program carefully and you'll soon find the mistake. Fixing errors (or bugs) is a bonus super skill that you'll build as you read this book!

**HANDY TIP!**
Keep a notebook for all your game ideas. Sketch out ideas for game characters, puzzles, and level designs the moment you think of them. Your notebook will be a huge help when you start to make your games!

# UNDERSTANDING CODING

To understand coding, we first need to know what coding is. Coding is all about creating instructions and information for computers using a language they can understand, which is often called "code." You rarely see computer code, but it's always there in the background making everything possible.

For example, when you draw a picture, the code tells the computer what to do when you move the mouse, what the different buttons on the screen do, how to draw a square, and so on. When you play a game, the code tells the computer what the rules of the game are, how to move your character and enemies, and what to do when you win or lose. The instructions can be incredibly detailed.

Code is also in many household machines, telling the tiny computer processors inside what they should do. Your washing machine has code to control its timings. Your TV includes code for displaying the interactive program guide. A cell phone and tablet are just different forms of a computer, so they also rely on code. How many more devices can you think of that might include code?

# COMPUTER LANGUAGES

There are tons of different computer languages. When used for writing instructions, they're usually called "programming languages." A program is a set of instructions that makes a computer do something.

Sometimes computer languages are used for organizing information, rather than writing instructions. For example, HTML is used to tell computers what the different parts of a web page are. This code doesn't tell the computer how to do anything, so it's not really a programming language. It's still a computer language, though, and it's still code.

THE BEST WAY TO LEARN TO CODE IS BY **DOING IT!**

# WHICH LANGUAGE?

There are lots of different programming languages. The one you choose depends firstly on which languages your computer or device can understand, and secondly on which language is best for the program you want to write. Programming languages are similar to human languages (such as English, Spanish, or Japanese) because they have different ways of saying more or less the same thing. They are different, though, in that programming languages are often particularly good at certain types of tasks.

Some popular programming languages include:

### SCRATCH

This is great for making games and programs that use a lot of pictures. It's easy for anyone to use.

### PYTHON

This language is easy for anyone to learn but it is powerful too. It's used to coordinate the special effects programs at Industrial Light & Magic, which was used for the *Harry Potter* and *Pirates of the Caribbean* films.

### C++

This language is often used for making programs that need to work extremely fast, including 3-D computer games.

### JAVA

This language is used for making games and other apps for Android cellular phones, and is often used inside devices such as air conditioning systems.

### JAVASCRIPT

This language is used to make interactive features for websites, such as menus that fly open, text that changes, or even online games. It's very different from Java, despite the similar names.

# HELLO WORLD!

To get a quick idea of how a computer language works, programmers often write a simple program to display the words "Hello World!" on the screen. Here's what it looks like in the languages we've just explored:

## SCRATCH

```
when        clicked
say   Hello World!   for   2   secs
```

## PYTHON

```
print("Hello World!")
```

You can probably see some differences and similarities between the languages above. Python and JavaScript don't look that different. Java and C++ use different instructions, though, and need a lot of additional code around the instruction that puts something on the screen.

When you look at the code, you can see how easy it can be to make a mistake. If you use the wrong type of bracket, put an instruction in the wrong place or leave out a semicolon, the program often won't work. Computers need everything to be precisely right, and they don't cope well with human error.

## C++

```cpp
#include <iostream>
int main()
{
    std::cout << "Hello World!";
}
```

## JAVA

```java
public class HelloWorld {
    public static void main(String[] args) {
        System.out.println("Hello, world!");
    }
}
```

## JAVASCRIPT

```javascript
alert("Hello World!");
```

AFTER YOU'VE LEARNED HOW TO BUILD A SCRATCH PROGRAM (SEE CHAPTER 2), YOU CAN COME BACK HERE AND TRY BUILDING THE EXAMPLE ON PAGE 9 TO CHECK WHETHER YOU GUESSED RIGHT!

**HANDY TIP!**
You sometimes need to install extra software to write using a programming language, but this software is often free. Make sure you get permission from the computer owner before installing any new software.

## MEET YOUR NEW LANGUAGES

In this book, we're going to use three computer languages: Scratch, HTML, and CSS. You won't need to install any extra software, but you will need a PC, Mac, or Linux computer that has an Internet connection.

Using Scratch, you'll learn about some of the most important ideas in programming. A lot of these ideas also matter in other programming languages. Many languages have a way of positioning things on the screen, repeating code, and storing information, so the super skills you learn here will also be valuable when you try other programming languages later.

Scratch is a great choice as your first programming language. Instead of having to type in instructions, they are provided as blocks, and you lock them together to build your program (or "script," in Scratch jargon). That means you're less likely to make mistakes when typing things in. You can also get quick results from Scratch that look great.

Here's an example Scratch program—a sneak preview of what your Scratch code will look like. The computer works its way through the instructions starting at the top. In Scratch, the instructions look a lot like a human language and use words that you will recognize. Can you work out what this program might do?

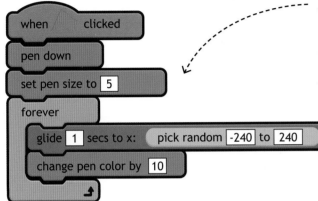

## BUILDING A WEBSITE

Another important skill is building a website to showcase your fantastic Scratch games. In the last two chapters, you'll learn two other computer languages: HTML and CSS. They're used together to build websites. You'll need to be very careful getting the brackets in the right places to make sure your website works correctly.

### HANDY TIP!

One way to test programs is to pretend to be the computer and follow the instructions yourself in your head. Predicting what a program will do is a valuable skill to develop, because it helps you fix errors faster.

Hello World!

# MASTERING YOUR TOOLS

Before you can write your game, you need to learn how to use the tools that help you build your programs. In this chapter, you'll get started with Scratch, make your first program, and try out the art editor and sound library.

## GETTING STARTED

Fire up your computer's web browser to the Scratch website (scratch.mit.edu). Click on "Join Scratch" at the top of the screen. You need to create a username and password. The username should be different from your real name (to protect your privacy), and the password should be something that's hard for others to guess. You also need to enter your birth month and year, gender, country, and email address. Some of this information is used by the Scratch team to understand who's using Scratch, and some of it helps you recover your password if you forget it.

Click on "Create" at the top of the screen. Now you're ready to start coding!

If you're logged in, Scratch will save your work automatically. To find your programs again later, click your username at the top right corner, and then click "My Stuff."

**Join Scratch**

It's easy (and free!) to sign up for a Scratch account

Choose a Scratch Username

Choose a Password

Confirm Password

Profile

My Stuff

Account settings

Sign out

**BE SAFE!**
ALWAYS ASK PERMISSION FROM AN ADULT BEFORE GIVING OUT ANY INFORMATION ABOUT YOURSELF ONLINE.

**HANDY TIP!**
You can try Scratch without becoming a member—just click on "Create" at the top of the screen. Before you spend too much time making anything, though, it's a good idea to sign up so you can save your work online.

# ACTION!

Creating your game is like directing a play or a film, and some of the words that are used are the same. The **Stage** is where the action happens. You'll learn how to move characters around on it soon.

**Sprites** are like the actors and props in a play. Racing cars, horses, and aliens would all be sprites. Even things that don't usually move, such as fences or trees, can be sprites. You can find your sprites in the **Sprite List** underneath the Stage.

In a play, **Scripts** are the lines the actors read. In a Scratch program, scripts are the instructions you give to your sprites. You can make sprites say things, but you can also tell them to make a sound, move around, draw a picture, or change what they look like. You make your scripts in the **Scripts Area**.

The **Backdrop** is the picture behind the sprites. For example, to make sprites look like they're in space, use a backdrop with a picture of stars on it.

Stage    Backdrop    Sprites    Scripts Area    A Script

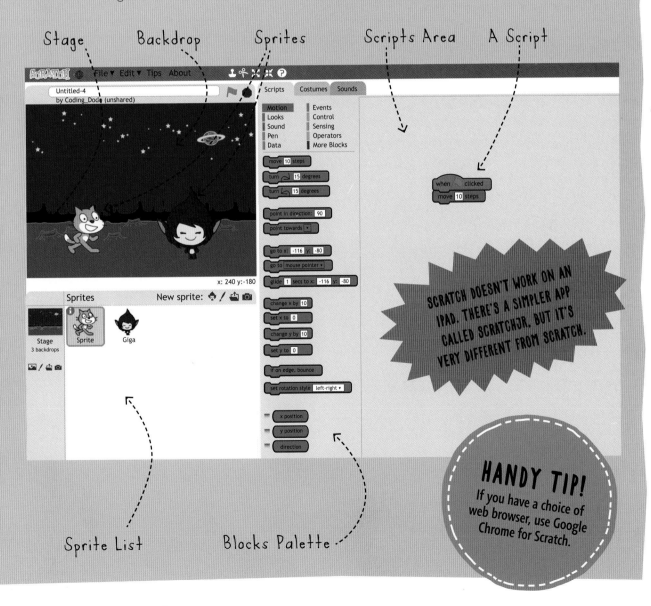

Sprite List    Blocks Palette

SCRATCH DOESN'T WORK ON AN IPAD. THERE'S A SIMPLER APP CALLED SCRATCHJR, BUT IT'S VERY DIFFERENT FROM SCRATCH.

**HANDY TIP!**
If you have a choice of web browser, use Google Chrome for Scratch.

# MAKING THE MARATHON CAT SCRIPT

OK, so now that you know where everything is on the screen and you have a Scratch account set up, you're ready to make your first script, called Marathon Cat. Every new project has the cat in it, so it stars in many Scratch projects.

The instructions that you use in Scratch are called blocks, and they lock together like jigsaw pieces. You can find them in the Blocks Palette, which is between the Stage and the Scripts Area. Click the Move 10 steps block, and you'll see the cat move.

move [ 10 ] steps

### HANDY TIP!
The 10 steps block tells the cat how far to move, not how many times, so you'll just see it move once. Click the 10 and type different numbers, and then click the block again. What happens?

## DRAGGING IN A BLOCK

Click the block, hold down the mouse button, and move the mouse over the Scripts Area. Release the mouse button, and the block will drop in the Scripts Area. You can now click the block in the Scripts Area to make the cat move.

### HANDY TIP!
This mouse movement is called "click and drag," and is used a lot for moving blocks and scripts around in Scratch.

# MAKING YOUR PROGRAM

The blocks are organized in 10 different color-coded categories. The `Move 10 steps` block is a Motion block because it moves a sprite. Click the "Events" button above the Blocks Palette, and you'll see a whole new set of brown blocks appear in the Blocks Palette. These blocks enable scripts to react when things happen.

Drag the `When green flag clicked` block from the Blocks Palette and drop it at the top of your `Move 10 steps` block in the Scripts Area. They should snap together.

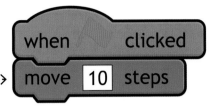

Congratulations! You've made your first script! It makes the cat move whenever you click the green flag button above the Stage. Try it!

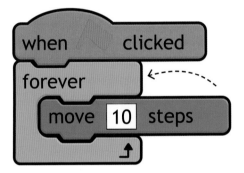

# MAKING THE CAT SPRINT

Let's make the cat keep moving without having to nudge it every step of the way. Click the "Control" button above the Blocks Palette, and find the `Forever` block. Drag it into your Scripts Area, and drop it around your `Move 10 steps` block. Anything inside the forever block repeats until you stop the program, using the red button above the Stage or an instruction in your program. Click the green flag button to see your cat run a marathon!

WHEN THE CAT RACES OFF THE SCREEN, YOU CAN CLICK AND DRAG IT BACK ONTO THE STAGE.

# EXPERIMENTATION TIME

Why not try adding other Motion and Looks blocks to see what they do? You can drag out the `Forever` block again, or put more things inside it. Experiment!

# POLISHING THE GRAPHICS

Let's change the backdrop. To the left of the Sprite List is a small icon for the backdrop. Underneath it are four icons for adding a new backdrop. Click the first icon, a landscape picture, to open the library. You can select from different categories and themes and use the scrollbar on the right to view more. Choose one of the pictures that includes pavement, and then drag the cat on the Stage into position. Click the cat in the Sprite List and then the Scripts tab to get back to your code.

## THERE AND BACK AGAIN

Add the `If on edge, bounce` block to your program and the cat will turn around when it reaches the edge of the screen and run back again.

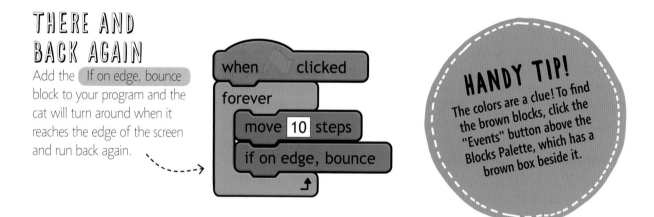

**HANDY TIP!**
The colors are a clue! To find the brown blocks, click the "Events" button above the Blocks Palette, which has a brown box beside it.

## FIXING YOUR FIRST BUG

Oh no! When the cat turns around and faces left, it flips on its head. This is a "bug," or mistake, in our program. Scratch follows our instructions exactly, but sometimes we have to be more precise to avoid strange things like this from happening. Fixing errors is called "debugging," and it's a big part of daily life for professional programmers.

To fix this bug, we need to use a block that changes the way the cat rotates. It's a Motion block called `set rotation style to left-right`. We only need to do this once, so we can put it outside our `Forever` block.

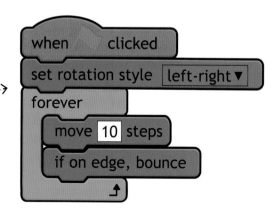

# ADDING SOUNDS

Add this script to your sprite. It doesn't connect to the movement script, but it still goes in the Scripts Area. Now, when you press the space bar, the cat makes a meow sound. Try it!

To add new sounds to your sprite, click the "Sounds" tab above the Blocks Palette. Click the small speaker (there are two!) where the Blocks Palette used to be. The library opens so you can find a sound and add it to your sprite. To play the sound in your program, use the play sound meow block, and click the drop-down menu in the block where it says "meow" to choose a different sound.

```
when  space ▼  key pressed
play sound  meow ▼
```

# USING THE ART EDITOR

Another idea Scratch has borrowed from the theater is the "costume." This is a picture of what the sprite looks like. Click the "Costumes" tab above the Blocks Palette, and you will see the cat's two costumes. There are two types of pictures, called "vectors" and "bitmaps." Bitmaps are easier to edit, so click on "Convert to Bitmap" in the bottom right corner.

On the left-hand side of the screen you will find a set of painting tools. Click a tool, then click a color at the bottom, and then use the mouse to draw on the cat sprite. For the line, rectangle, and ellipse tools, click and drag the mouse to make a shape. The "Select" tool enables you to choose part of your picture to move or duplicate (copy); it works using "click and drag" too. For the brush and erase tools, click the button and move the mouse to draw or erase.

### SCRATCH PAINTING TOOLS

- Brush
- Line
- Rectangle
- Ellipse
- Text
- Fill with color
- Erase
- Select
- Select and duplicate

# PRACTICE MAKES PERFECT!

Now you know how to make scripts, change the backdrop, add sounds, and edit the sprite's costume. Spend some time honing your skills with your new tools.

# GETTING YOUR BEARINGS

Whether a player wins or loses a game might depend on the precise position of their sprite, the enemies, and the obstacles. One of the super skills you'll need is an understanding of how the screen is organized and how you can put your sprites exactly where you want them.

## UNDERSTANDING GRID COORDINATES

Scratch uses coordinates to control where sprites are positioned on the Stage. The "X" coordinate is used for the horizontal position (from left to right), and the "Y" coordinate is used for the vertical position (from top to bottom). If you've drawn graphs or used maps before, you'll be familiar with this idea.

When you start a new Scratch project, the cat is in the middle of the screen. The coordinates are all measured from the middle of the screen, so this is where X and Y are both zero. Positions to the left of the center have a negative X value (for example, -10), and those to the right have a positive number (for example, 10). For the Y coordinates, negative numbers are below the center and positive numbers are above the center.

There's a backdrop included with Scratch that makes it much easier to see how the coordinates work. It's called an XY-grid, and you can find it by going into the backdrop library and clicking the "Other" category. Start a new project and add that backdrop. If you can't remember how to change backdrops, go back to Chapter 2.

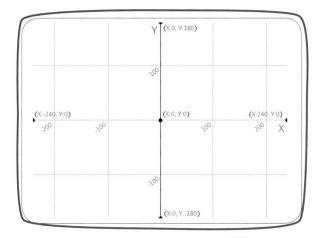

**HANDY TIP!**
Here's an easy way to remember the difference between X and Y: "X is across." It's memorable because "x" is also a cross shape.

# CHANGING A SPRITE'S POSITION

There are six Motion blocks that use coordinates to change a sprite's position. When you click the number in a block, you can type in a new number, either negative or positive.

This block moves the sprite to a specific coordinate. Use x:0 y:0 to return a sprite to the center, or change the numbers to put it somewhere else. The sprite jumps there immediately.

Want to watch the sprite move into place? Use this block instead. The 1 secs part means the movement will take 1 second. You can use 0.5 for half a second to speed it up.

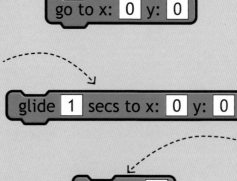

You can set a sprite's X coordinate to a particular position without affecting its Y coordinate. Using this block with a value of 0 puts the sprite in the middle of the screen horizontally, but doesn't affect how far up or down the screen it is.

This block changes the Y coordinate, without affecting the X coordinate. To drop a sprite to the bottom of the screen without changing its x position, use this block with a value of -150.

This block will change the X position, relative to where the sprite already is. Use change x by -50 to take a big leap left, or change x by 10 for a small step to the right.

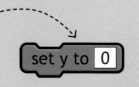

Use this block to change the Y position without changing the X position. For example, use change y by 20 to make the sprite jump up the screen, or change y by -20 to drop it down.

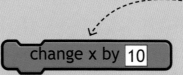

BEWARE! THE SET AND CHANGE BLOCKS DO VERY DIFFERENT JOBS. BUT THEY'RE EASILY CONFUSED.

# PIN THE TAIL ON THE DONKEY

Super skills come with practice, so here's a simple game to help you fine-tune your instinct for screen positions. It's based on the party game "Pin the Tail on the Donkey," where a player is blindfolded and has to pin a paper tail to a picture of a donkey. The winner is the one who gets closest to the right place. Our game is a digital version, where you place the tail by setting its coordinates. How close can you get?

## HOW TO MAKE THE GAME

**1** Start a new project. Right-click the cat to open the menu, and choose "Delete". We don't need it this time.

**2** Above the Sprite List are four buttons to add new sprites. Click the first one to choose a sprite from the library and pick Horse1. You'll find it faster if you go into the "Animals" category on the left first.

**3** Right-click the horse (either on the Stage or in the Sprite List) to open the menu and choose "Duplicate." Now you have two horses.

**4** Click the first horse in the Sprite List, and click the "Costumes" tab. In the art editor, click the "Convert to Bitmap" button. Then use the eraser to delete the horse's tail.

**HANDY TIP!**
If you find the game too hard, try adding the XY-grid backdrop and use that to work out the tail's position.

**5** Click the second horse in the Sprite List. This time, use the art editor to delete the horse's body so only the tail remains. Now that we've erased a lot of the costume, we also need to tell Scratch where the middle of it should be. Click the cross button in the top right to change the costume center, and then click on the middle of the tail. If you don't do this, the tail's position will be wrong in the game, because Scratch will think the middle of the tail is where the horse's body used to be.

**HANDY TIP!**

ask What's your name? and wait and answer are both Sensing blocks. You need to change the question in the ask block and drag the answer block on top of the set x to 0 and set y to 0 blocks.

**6** Click the "Scripts" tab above the Blocks Palette, and then click the horse body in the Sprite list to make this script for it. The pick random 1 to 10 block, an "Operator" block, chooses a random number for you and is used here to put the horse in a random position. The numbers shown here will put the horse randomly somewhere on the screen with enough room for the tail to be added. When you change a sprite's X or Y position, it's actually the middle of the sprite that sits at the point you specify. If we put the horse too close to the edge of the Stage, its head, legs, or behind will spill off the Stage.

**7** Click the tail in the Sprite List and give it this script. The answer and ask blocks are Sensing blocks.

**8** Click the green flag, and see how closely you can position the tail! Each time you play, the body is in a new position.

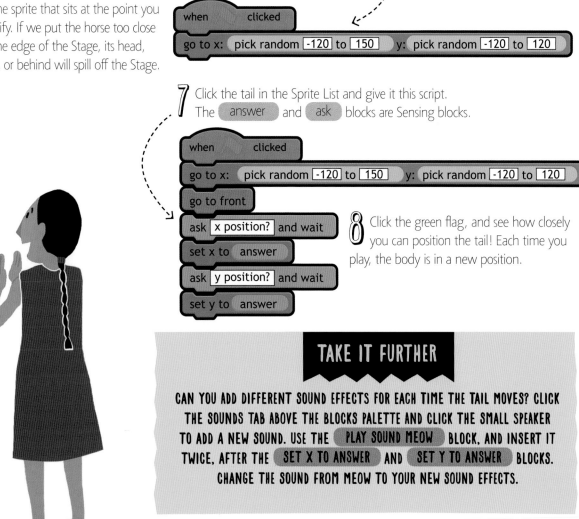

**TAKE IT FURTHER**

CAN YOU ADD DIFFERENT SOUND EFFECTS FOR EACH TIME THE TAIL MOVES? CLICK THE SOUNDS TAB ABOVE THE BLOCKS PALETTE AND CLICK THE SMALL SPEAKER TO ADD A NEW SOUND. USE THE PLAY SOUND MEOW BLOCK, AND INSERT IT TWICE, AFTER THE SET X TO ANSWER AND SET Y TO ANSWER BLOCKS. CHANGE THE SOUND FROM MEOW TO YOUR NEW SOUND EFFECTS.

# DRAWING WITH THE PEN

The Pen blocks enable you to draw pictures on the Stage by moving sprites around it. When a sprite's pen is down, it leaves a line everywhere it goes. You can change the size and color of the pen and use the `clear` block to erase your picture from the Stage. To stop the sprite from drawing as it moves, use the `pen up` block.

Using the pen is another great way to get your bearings on the Stage. Start a new project, and add the XY-grid backdrop. Click the cat sprite and add the following script to it. Click the green flag to see the cat draw a boat.

```
when [flag] clicked
clear
set pen color to [■]
set pen size to 8
pen up
go to x: -100 y: -100
pen down
go to x: -150 y: -50
go to x: 150 y: -50
go to x: 100 y: -100
go to x: -100 y: -100
pen up
go to x: -50 y: -50
pen down
go to x: -50 y: 0
go to x: 0 y: 0
go to x: 0 y: -50
pen up
go to x: 100 y: -50
pen down
go to x: 100 y: 0
go to x: 150 y: 0
go to x: 150 y: -50
```

**HANDY TIP!**
The `set pen color to` block enables you to pick a color from the screen when you click the color box. Here we used a metallic gray, but you can pick something else.

In this picture, the cat has been dragged out of the way so that you can see the drawing clearly. The cat moves too quickly for you to follow on-screen, but can you work out which order the lines were drawn in? Take a look at the `go to x:0 y:0` blocks in the program and the XY-grid to trace the cat's path.

## WHY ARE THERE SO MANY "PEN UP" AND "PEN DOWN" BLOCKS?

Sometimes we want to move the cat to a new position without drawing a line, such as when we move to the starting point for one of the boat's chimneys. If we don't lift the pen first, we end up with lines where we don't want them.

**HANDY TIP!**
Each sprite has its own pen, so you can make some sprites draw while others don't.

# CHANGING THE BOAT'S POSITION

What if you wanted to move the boat 20 steps to the left? That's really hard, because you have to change all the X coordinates in the blocks. If you decide to change the Y coordinate too, that's even more editing to do.

That's why it's a good idea not to use particular coordinates, but to use the blocks you've already seen for changing the X or Y position or some new blocks for moving and changing direction (see box on the right).

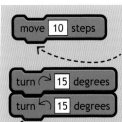

This moves a sprite a certain number of steps in the direction it is traveling. Remember that you can stop the sprite at any time by rotating it on the screen, even when it's traveling in a particular direction.

This turns a sprite's traveling direction by a certain number of degrees.

This turns the sprite to a particular traveling direction. 0 is up. Left is -90, right is 90 and down is 180. Use negative numbers (between 0 and -179) for counterclockwise directions, and positive numbers (0 to 180) for clockwise.

This script draws the base of the boat using directions instead, this time in green. Can you finish it by adding the chimneys? Now you can put the boat wherever you want!

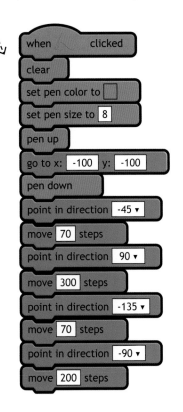

# ADDING THE SEA AND SKY

By drawing an extremely thick blue line under the boat, you can add the sea, and the sun can be added with a tiny line drawn with a giant pen. Finally, you can put the cat on top of the boat. Join these blocks to the end of your script so far.

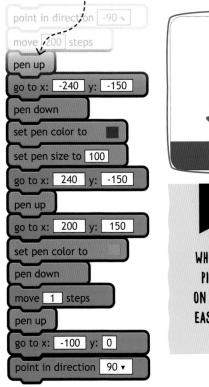

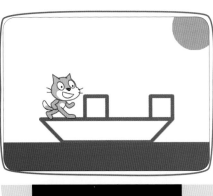

## TAKE IT FURTHER

WHY NOT TRY DRAWING YOUR OWN PICTURE? YOU CAN PLOT IT OUT ON GRAPH PAPER FIRST TO MAKE IT EASIER TO PLOT THE COORDINATES.

# DON'T REPEAT YOURSELF

Sometimes you might want to do the same thing over and over again, but it's boring to write a program with the same instructions in it (even if you copy and paste them!). Instead, you can use loops that tell the computer to repeat some of the instructions for you.

## DRAWING A SQUARE

To see how loops work, let's use an example of a simple script that draws a square each time you click the green flag. You can move the cat each time to stop it writing over the previous square.

```
when     clicked
pen down
move 50 steps
turn  90 degrees
move 50 steps
turn  90 degrees
move 50 steps
turn  90 degrees
move 50 steps
```

There are several problems with this script. The first is that it's difficult to work out what the program is going to do by reading it. The best programs are easy for anyone to understand. In this script, you'd have to check all the angles and sides to be sure it was going to draw a complete and perfect square.

The second problem is that it's tedious to create, having to drag in the same blocks over and over again. You can duplicate blocks (right-click on them to open the menu to do that), but it's still a good thing we aren't creating an octagon, nonagon, decagon, or a shape with even more sides!

If you wanted to change the script to draw a different shape, you would have to edit almost every block too.

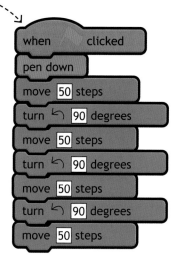

**HANDY TIP!**
Loops aren't just about drawing. You can use a loop for any part of the program you want to repeat.

# CREATING A LOOP

One of the guidelines of good programming is avoid repeating yourself. Instead, let the computer do the repetitive parts for you. One way to do that is by writing a loop, a small part of a program that is repeated multiple times.

In Scratch, you can use the `repeat 10` block to create a loop. In this case, you only need to repeat 4 times, so change the number in the block to a 4. The instructions inside the yellow `repeat 4` bracket are carried out 4 times. This script is shorter, quicker to build, and easier to understand.

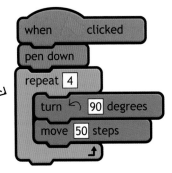

# EDITING YOUR LOOP

Another good thing about creating a loop is that it is easy to change. What if you decide to make a 10-sided shape (a decagon), instead? You only need to change two numbers. It certainly beats writing or editing separate instructions for every line you want to draw.

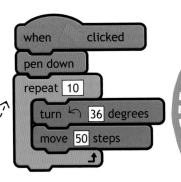

## HANDY TIP!

Can you modify the script to draw a triangle, a hexagon, or a pentagon? All you need to do is divide 360 by the number of sides to work out the angle of each corner.

# LOOPS INSIDE LOOPS

What if you want to make a pattern using 150 squares? You can put a loop that draws a square inside another loop that repeats 150 times. In this script, instructions were added telling the cat to move to a random location before drawing each square and changing the pen color before each one.

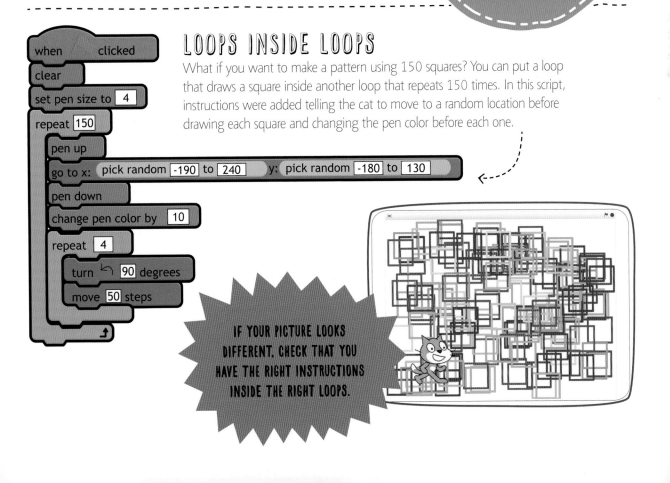

IF YOUR PICTURE LOOKS DIFFERENT, CHECK THAT YOU HAVE THE RIGHT INSTRUCTIONS INSIDE THE RIGHT LOOPS.

# CREATING YOUR OWN BLOCKS

Often you'll find that different parts of the program do similar jobs. For example, you might have a sprite that jumps when the player presses a button and also flies into the air when it touches a booster pad. To avoid repeating yourself, you can make one set of blocks that is used for both of these effects. The sprite might move to a different height and at a different speed for a jump and a boost, but you can still reuse the instructions. In Scratch, you do this by making your own blocks. To see how this works, let's make a block that draws squares.

Above the Blocks Palette, click the "More Blocks" button and then click the "Make a Block" button in the Blocks Palette. When the menu opens, it has an empty purple block in it. This is where you name your block. We'll call it "draw a square of size." Click "Options" and you will see different pieces of information that your block can use. We'll need a number, so click the button to add a number input. In the purple block above, you'll see a hole with "number1" in it. Click that word and change it to "square size."

The second thing that happens is a `define` block is added in the Scripts Area. This is where you tell Scratch what your new block should do, by building a script for it, as shown below. To add the `square size` block to your script, just drag it from the purple `define` block. It fits into the spot in the `move 10 steps` block. Here's the script for drawing a square.

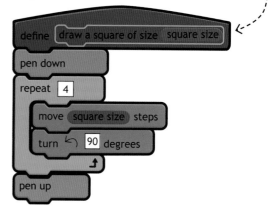

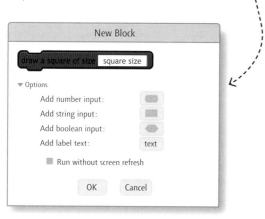

When you click "OK," two things happen. First, a new block appears in the Blocks Palette, which is the block you created. You can see it contains a spot for a number, like the spot in the `move 10 steps` block. The number you put in here also goes into your `square size` block, so you can include it in your instructions for the block.

Now you have a new command you can use to draw a square of any size anywhere. To draw a square that has sides that are 50 steps long, you would use this coding block.

## HANDY TIP!

Part of the skill of programming is spotting where you can break a program down into smaller parts like this. Look out for opportunities like this to reuse parts of your scripts.

# USING YOUR NEW BLOCK

Now we can use our square drawing block to write a script that draws a house, with squares used for the windows and the outline, and separate lines added for the roof (at the start) and the door (at the end). Despite the number of squares in the picture, we only have to tell Scratch how to draw a square once.

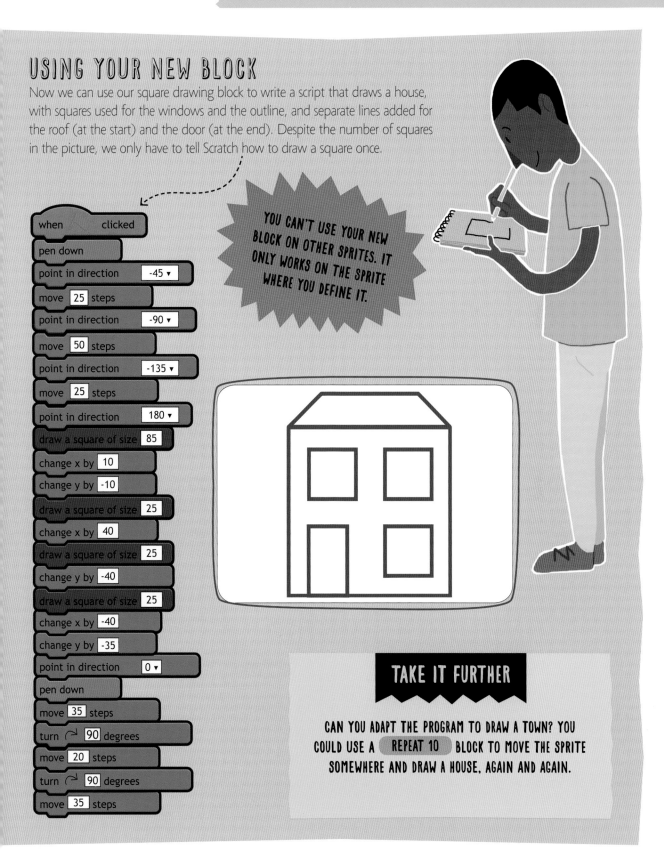

YOU CAN'T USE YOUR NEW BLOCK ON OTHER SPRITES. IT ONLY WORKS ON THE SPRITE WHERE YOU DEFINE IT.

```
when  clicked
pen down
point in direction  -45 ▾
move 25 steps
point in direction  -90 ▾
move 50 steps
point in direction  -135 ▾
move 25 steps
point in direction  180 ▾
draw a square of size 85
change x by 10
change y by -10
draw a square of size 25
change x by 40
draw a square of size 25
change y by -40
draw a square of size 25
change x by -40
change y by -35
point in direction  0 ▾
pen down
move 35 steps
turn ↻ 90 degrees
move 20 steps
turn ↻ 90 degrees
move 35 steps
```

## TAKE IT FURTHER

CAN YOU ADAPT THE PROGRAM TO DRAW A TOWN? YOU COULD USE A `REPEAT 10` BLOCK TO MOVE THE SPRITE SOMEWHERE AND DRAW A HOUSE, AGAIN AND AGAIN.

# MAKING DECISIONS

Sometimes programs need to make a decision about what to do next, depending on what else is going on in the program or what the user is doing. In this chapter, you'll learn how to write scripts that make decisions.

## MAKING THE BUZZER GAME

You might have seen the buzzer game at a fair, where you need a steady hand to guide a loop along a wiggly wire without touching it. Our first game in this chapter uses a similar idea. Guide an arrow around the screen, but don't touch the color red.

All our programs so far have done the same thing each time we've run them. The pictures we've drawn were the same each time we clicked the green flag, except for some random positions.

For this game, we need Scratch to do different things for us when we press keys to control our sprite, and we need it to sound the buzzer if we touch the forbidden color too. Each time the game runs, it can be played differently, with some players going in odd directions and some players touching the red more than others. The program needs to decide where and when to move the sprite and when to sound the buzzer.

The block you use for making decisions is the `if...then` block (see above right). The idea of this block might seem strange at first, but humans think like this too. Imagine the sentence "If it's raining, then put on your coat." The "it's raining" part is like the diamond-shaped part of the `if...then` block, and the "put your coat on" part would go inside the bracket.

### THE PARTS OF THE "IF...THEN" BLOCK

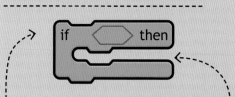

- A diamond-shaped area is used to decide whether the program should do something or not.

- A bracket, like the `repeat 10` block goes here. Inside this bracket go the instructions that might happen, or might not, depending on what the program decides.

BUZZ!
BUZZ!

# TRYING THE "IF...THEN" BLOCK

Here's a simple script to show the if...then block in action. It checks whether the space bar is pressed using one of the Sensing blocks, and if it is, it moves the sprite 10 steps. We have to use a forever block so that the program keeps checking whether we're pressing the space bar or not. Click the green flag, and the sprite will move when you press the space bar.

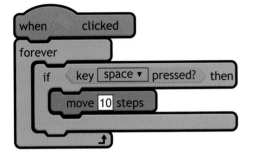

Often, you want to check whether one number is bigger, less than, or equal to another number. For example, you might want to check whether the sprite's X position is bigger than 240, which would mean it's off the right-hand side of the Stage. For comparisons like this, use some of the Operator blocks.

BUZZ!
BUZZ!
BUZZ!

## COMPARING NUMBERS WITH OPERATORS

The < block checks whether the number in the first box is less than the number in the second box, the = block checks if they're the same and the > block checks if the first one is larger than the second one.

For example: It moves the sprite when you press the space bar, but when it goes off the right side of the Stage, it puts it back on the left side.

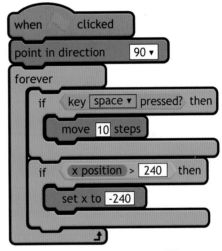

## HANDY TIP!

There are lots of other factors you can base your decisions on. Using the touching ? block, you can check whether a sprite is touching another sprite, the edge of the Stage, or the mouse pointer. You can check whether the mouse button is pressed using the mouse down block, and test whether a sprite is touching a particular color.

# CODING THE BUZZER GAME

Now you're ready to write the Buzzer game. First, design your backdrop. Under the Stage in the Sprite List, click the paintbrush to paint a new backdrop and decorate it with red obstacles to steer around. Right-click the cat sprite and choose "delete." Now add Arrow1 as a new sprite. Add the "buzz whir" sound effect to your Arrow1 sprite.

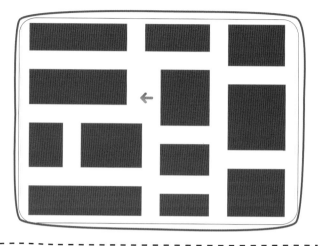

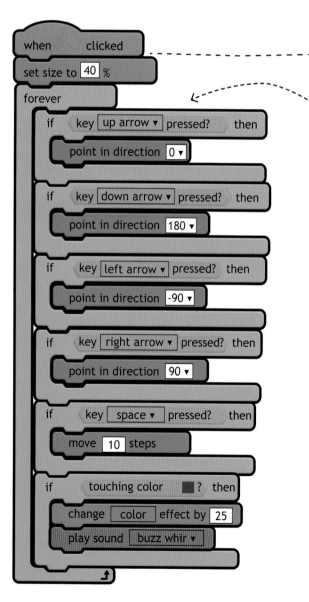

Here's the script you need to put on the Arrow1 sprite to enable you to play Buzzer.

There are a few new things here. For detecting the key presses, use the `key space pressed?` Sensing block and click the drop-down menu to change the key to something else. The `touching color?` block is also a Sensing block. To change the color in it to red, click the square in it and then click one of your obstacles on the Stage. That will ensure you match the shade of the obstacles exactly when checking whether the sprite is touching red.

You can also add a color-changing effect from the Looks blocks for when you hit the obstacle. Because the obstacle detection is in the `forever` loop, like the keyboard controls, the script keeps changing your sprite's color as long as you're touching an obstacle, making it strobe in different colors.

See if you can get from one side of the screen to the other. Perhaps play with a friend, and see who lasts longest without hitting an obstacle, or take turns when the arrow hits the red.

### HANDY TIP!

There is also an Events block, when space key pressed, which you can use to trigger a script when a key is pressed. It tends to be a tad too slow to use in action games, but this is another way you can control a sprite. It just goes to show that there are often two or more ways to write a program!

# ADJUSTING THE DIFFICULTY

If games are too difficult, they're frustrating and players give up. If games are too easy, there's no challenge and nobody's excited to play them. Finding the right difficulty level is tricky, but it's essential for making successful video games.

The way to get the difficulty right is to get somebody else to test your games. You can watch them while they play your version of Buzzer and see which parts are too hard. Because you've built the game, you'll probably find the game easier than anyone else, but resist the urge to help them!

In addition to watching how they play, make sure there's enough space for players to get between all the obstacles. It's not fair if the gap isn't big enough. In the second block of this example script, the size of the sprite is set to 40 percent, but you can make your sprite smaller if the obstacles are closer together. Just make sure the sprite doesn't get too small for others to see.

## TAKE IT FURTHER

YOU CAN ALSO ADD A COLORED TARGET SPRITE FOR THE PLAYER TO REACH AND MAKE A TRIUMPHANT SOUND WHEN THE ARROW IS TOUCHING IT. YOU CAN ALSO DESIGN DIFFERENT BACKDROPS SO THERE ARE DIFFERENT PATHS TO NAVIGATE. WHAT ELSE CAN YOU DO TO IMPROVE THIS GAME?

# USING THE "IF...THEN...ELSE" BLOCK

There's another block you can use for making decisions, the `if...then...else` block. You can think of the word "else" as meaning "otherwise," so use this block for decisions like "If it's raining, then wear a coat, otherwise wear sunglasses."

## TRYING IT OUT

Here's a simple example that you can use on any sprite. Click the menu in the `touching ?` block to select mouse-pointer. The `say` block (one of the Looks blocks) uses a speech bubble to display a message. It stays there until the sprite says something else. If you use the block with nothing in the text box, the speech bubble disappears. This script makes the sprite say something when you touch it with the mouse, but stops when the mouse pointer isn't touching it anymore.

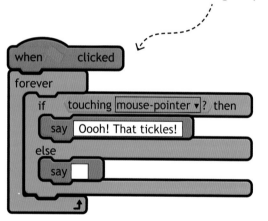

## THE PARTS OF THE "IF...THEN...ELSE" BLOCK

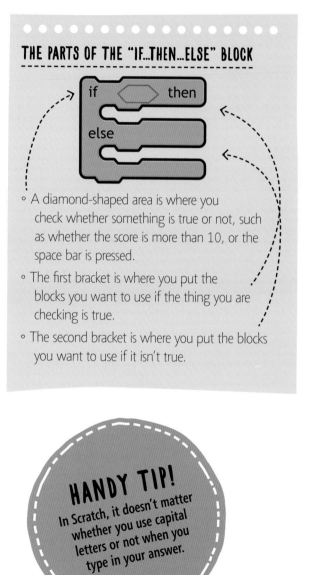

- A diamond-shaped area is where you check whether something is true or not, such as whether the score is more than 10, or the space bar is pressed.
- The first bracket is where you put the blocks you want to use if the thing you are checking is true.
- The second bracket is where you put the blocks you want to use if it isn't true.

**HANDY TIP!**
In Scratch, it doesn't matter whether you use capital letters or not when you type in your answer.

# ASKING QUESTIONS

In a moment you'll see how to build a quiz game. Before that, we need to work out how we get the player to type something in. The `ask "What's your name?"` block, which is one of the Sensing blocks, enables you to ask a question and opens a panel for the player to type their answer in. Whatever they type is stored in the `answer` block. You've already seen these blocks in Chapter 3, but now you need to really understand how they work.

Programmers often make short test programs like this to see how (and whether!) something works or not. Once you've tried this, you can right-click this script and delete it.

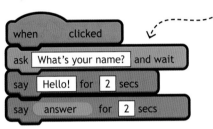

# MAKING A QUIZ GAME

For the quiz, you can use any backdrop and any sprite to ask the questions. First, make a short animation to celebrate when the player gets a question right. Create a block called `victory dance` for this. In this example, the whoop sound effect has been added to the sprite, using the "Sounds" tab.

The question script brings together lots of things you learned in this chapter. It asks a quiz question. It uses the `=` block to see whether the answer typed in is equal to (or the same as) the right answer, China. If so, it does a victory dance. If not, it shows the right answer instead.

To add another question, right-click on the `ask` block and choose "duplicate" from the menu. Scratch copies all the blocks under the `ask` block too. Simply join them to the bottom of your script and edit them for the new question and answer. You can keep adding more and more questions.

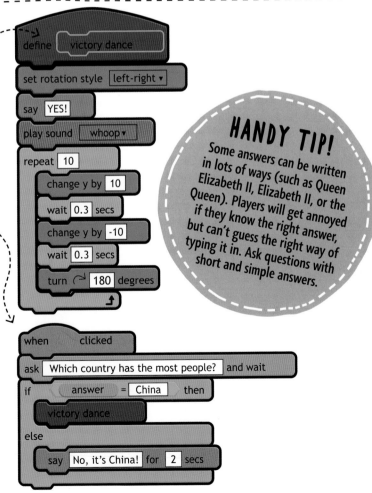

**HANDY TIP!**
Some answers can be written in lots of ways (such as Queen Elizabeth II, Elizabeth II, or the Queen). Players will get annoyed if they know the right answer, but can't guess the right way of typing it in. Ask questions with short and simple answers.

# USING VARIABLES

Whether it's names, scores, or quiz questions, computers store all kinds of information. In this chapter, you'll learn how to use variables and lists to keep track of the information in your games.

## MAKING A VARIABLE

If you want to remember a piece of information in a game, you can use a variable. A variable is like a box for storing information, either a number or a piece of text. It's called a variable because the information in it can vary (or change). During a game, the number in the score variable might go up or down, for example.

To make a variable in Scratch, click the Data button above the Blocks Palette and then click the "Make a Variable" button in the Blocks Palette. Enter a name for your variable, such as "score."

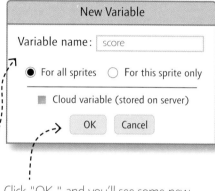

New Variable

Variable name: score

● For all sprites    ○ For this sprite only

☐ Cloud variable (stored on server)

OK    Cancel

Click "OK," and you'll see some new blocks appear in the Blocks Palette.

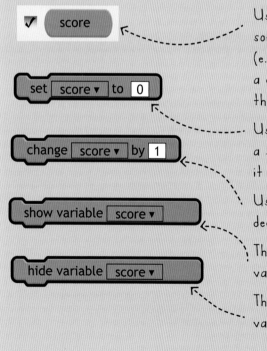

Use this block whenever you want to do something with the number inside the variable (e.g. to see whether the score is high enough for a congratulations message.) The tick box shows the variable on the Stage.

Use this block to set the value of the score to a specific number. At the start of the game, use it to reset the score.

Use this block to increase the score or decrease it by using a negative number.

This block displays the variable on the Stage.

This block hides the variable on the Stage.

**HANDY TIP!**
Use variable names that help you remember what you're storing in the variable.

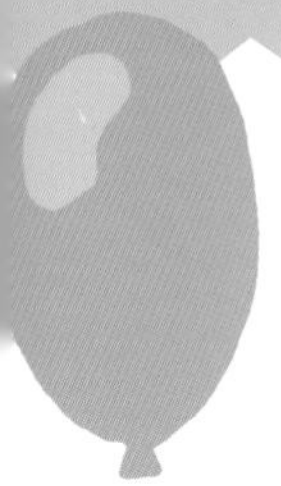

# CREATING THE BALLOON POPPER GAME

Here's a game to show you how to keep score. Balloons float up the screen. Each time you click one, it disappears and the score increases by one.

Start a new project, delete the cat sprite, and add the balloon sprite. Make a new variable called "score," and add the "triumph" music to the sprite. You will need to use the two scripts shown on the right.

The main script sets the score to zero at the start. Then it starts a loop that repeats 10 times. Each time, it puts a balloon at a random point at the bottom of the screen and moves it gradually to the top. At the end, if the score is more than 8, it plays a triumphant jingle. The other script increases the score and hides the balloon when it is clicked.

```
when  clicked
set score ▾ to 0
repeat 10
    go to x: pick random -240 to 240   y: -180
    show
    repeat 48
        change y by 10
if  score > 8  then
    play sound triumph ▾
```

```
when this sprite clicked
change score ▾ by 1
hide
```

## HANDY TIP!

To play, click the "Full Screen" button above the Stage, beside the project name. Otherwise, Scratch might think you're trying to reposition sprites on the Stage.

FOR THE IF BLOCK IN THE MAIN SCRIPT, DRAG IN THE BLOCKS IN THIS ORDER: IF , > , SCORE .

## TAKE IT FURTHER

CHANGE THE NUMBERS SO EACH CLICK SCORES 10 POINTS AND THE JINGLE PLAYS WHEN THE PLAYER GETS MORE THAN 50 POINTS.

# USING TEXT WITH VARIABLES

The `answer` block only keeps track of the last thing that was typed in. If you put the information in a variable, you can use it whenever you like later on.

In this simple example, the sprite remembers your name, even after you've typed in your home town. Remember to make the variables "player name" and "home town" before trying to use them. Click the variable name menu in the `set` block to choose a different variable when there's more than one. The green `join` block enables you to put two pieces of text in the same speech bubble. Put a space after "hello" to avoid the text running together.

## ALL OR ONE, ONE OR ALL?

When you make a variable, you're asked whether you'd like to make it for one sprite or all sprites. Usually, it's okay to make the variable for all sprites.

Making a variable for just one sprite is sometimes a good idea for two reasons. Firstly, it protects the variable from bugs caused by other sprites changing it when they shouldn't. Lots of programming languages use this idea to make programs more reliable and easier to debug. Secondly, it means you can duplicate a sprite, and its variables will still work as you expect. That's because several sprites can have the same variables as long as the variable was created only for that sprite. You might have an alien sprite that uses an "energy" variable, for example. If you make that variable for only one sprite, you can duplicate the sprite, and both sprites will have their own "energy" variables that work independently.

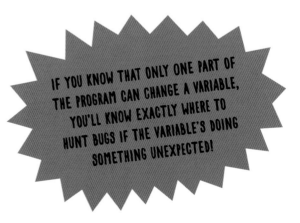

IF YOU KNOW THAT ONLY ONE PART OF THE PROGRAM CAN CHANGE A VARIABLE, YOU'LL KNOW EXACTLY WHERE TO HUNT BUGS IF THE VARIABLE'S DOING SOMETHING UNEXPECTED!

## GIVE IT A GO!

Try this simple program to see how it works. Start a new project and add the Sun sprite. Make the variable "energy" for only this sprite. Now add these scripts to your sprite.

When you click the green flag, you'll see the sprite's energy is 100 on the Stage. When you click the sprite, its energy goes down by 1.

Right-click the sprite in the Sprite List and choose "Duplicate" so you have two suns on the Stage. Now click the green flag, and you'll see two energy variables on the Stage: one for Sun and one for Sun2. When you click one of the sprites, its energy value goes down without affecting the other sprite.

You can duplicate the sprite to add even more suns. For many games, using this technique enables you to make one enemy sprite and then make copies for all the others, without having to change the code for each one.

```
when     clicked
set  energy ▾  to  100
show variable  energy ▾
```

```
when this sprite clicked
change  energy ▾  by  -1
```

**HANDY TIP!**
This technique is ideal when you want to duplicate sprites without messing up the other variables.

# USING LISTS

You can only store one number or piece of text in a variable. You can use more than one variable in a program, but there's a better way to store a group of similar items, called a list.

To make a list, click the "Data" button above the Blocks Palette, and then click the "Make a List" button. Give it a name (let's start with a list called "friends") and click "OK." You'll see some new blocks in the Blocks Palette that you can use for adding items to your list, deleting items from it, inserting items at a particular point in the list, and replacing one item with another item. There are also blocks that enable you to look at one of your list items or check whether an item is on the list.

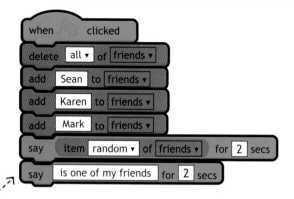

Here's a simple program that builds a list of friends and then talks about one of them, chosen at random.

The program starts by emptying the list (using the `delete 1 of friends` block and changing the "1" to "all"), otherwise it gets longer every time you click the green flag. Use the `add thing to friends` block to add friends to the list. The `item 1 of friends` block has a menu in it you can use to choose a random item. Try typing different numbers in this space, and experiment with adding more names.

## STREAMLINING THE QUIZ

Remember our quiz game in the last chapter? Let's improve it by using lists to store the questions and answers. Create a variable called "question number," a list called "questions," and another list called "answers." Then create the script on the left. It looks quite complicated, but it uses blocks and ideas you've seen before.

The "question number" variable is used to remember which round of the quiz we're in (question 1, 2, or 3 in this quiz). The first time around, its value is 1. So the program asks question 1, and then checks the player's answer against the first item in the answer list. At the end of the loop, the question number increases, so the next time around, it asks question 2.

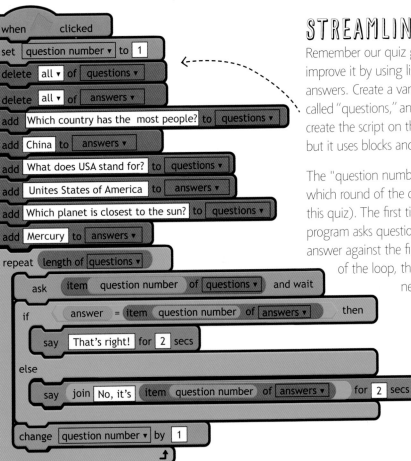

```
when [] clicked
set question number ▾ to 1
delete all ▾ of questions ▾
delete all ▾ of answers ▾
add Which country has the most people? to questions ▾
add China to answers ▾
add What does USA stand for? to questions ▾
add Unites States of America to answers ▾
add Which planet is closest to the sun? to questions ▾
add Mercury to answers ▾
repeat length of questions ▾
    ask item question number of questions ▾ and wait
    if answer = item question number of answers ▾ then
        say That's right! for 2 secs
    else
        say join No, it's item question number of answers ▾ for 2 secs
    change question number ▾ by 1
```

### HANDY TIP!

The main loop is a `repeat 10` block with the `length of questions` block in the space where the number would usually go.

## WHY IS THIS WAY BEST?

In the last chapter you saw how to make a quiz by duplicating blocks. This program is much easier to understand and update. All the questions and answers are in one place, and you can change the game behavior by modifying the main game loop.

### TAKE IT FURTHER

CAN YOU PUT THE VICTORY DANCE IN AND ADD A SCORE THAT INCREASES WHEN THE PLAYER GETS AN ANSWER RIGHT? TRY ADDING MORE QUESTIONS AND ANSWERS TO THIS QUIZ (BEFORE THE `REPEAT` BLOCK).

# PLANNING YOUR GAME

Now that you've mastered the basics of coding, you're ready to plan a game. It's time to think about the theme of your game and to start testing some of the code you'll need.

## CHOOSING A THEME

In the next chapter, you'll make a platform game, where your character has to leap onto platforms and avoid enemies.

Before you start building your game, think about where you'll set it. Whether it's in space, on the farm, or on the streets, it will affect the sprites you use and the background images. You could make a fantasy game that combines aliens, cows, and trains, but your game will make more sense to players if you have one theme and stick to it.

In this example game, Treetop Catnap, the cat wants to nap in a tree, but it must first find its way to the tree house. That means jumping from branch to branch and dodging the biting insects that drain its energy.

Start by gathering or drawing some sprites you can use for your game. You'll need a character for the player to move and an enemy to avoid. You can also design a backdrop. Don't worry about spending too long on the graphics yet. Programmers often use rough images while building their game, and then add the real graphics later so they can get into programming right away. As they develop the game, they might have better ideas for the graphics too.

## USING PROTOTYPES

Programmers often build "prototypes," which are simple, early versions of a program that allow them to test how things work. These prototypes are used for the most important parts of the program and for the parts that will be the most difficult to write. If they don't work, the programmer has more time to work out a way to fix them or to consider alternative game ideas.

### HANDY TIP!

Want to star in your game? Why not upload a photo of yourself? Go to the Costumes tab of a sprite and click the folder icon at the top.

SHORT OF IDEAS? THINK ABOUT YOUR FAVORITE BOOKS AND FILMS. WHERE WERE THEY SET? WHAT WERE THE MOST EXCITING ADVENTURES?

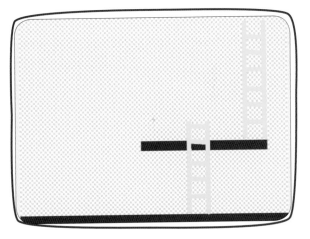

# PROTOTYPING A LEVEL DESIGN

For you to do some testing, you need to create a simple level design that you can experiment with. We're going to use different colors to tell whether something can be stood on (a platform), can be climbed (a rope or ladder), or is the final goal (the tree house in this game). In this example, red is used for platforms and yellow is used for the ladders. The goal will be brown.

It is best to design your levels by creating a new sprite and drawing a costume for it. You can make this sprite big enough to fill the Stage. This way, you'll be able to extend and shorten platforms in your sprite costume without making a mess of the background. Click the "paintbrush" icon above the Sprite List to start. Click and drag your sprite onto the Stage if necessary so you can see it all. Later on, you can put a backdrop behind it to make the screen layout more interesting.

# PROTOTYPING GRAVITY

If the player's character falls off a platform, it should fall until it reaches another platform. We'll need to test whether the player is on firm footing or floating through the air in our game, so let's make a block to check for this.

Click the cat in the Sprite List. In the Blocks Palette, click on "More Blocks" and make a new block called "Check Footing." We'll use a variable called "am I floating" to remember whether the sprite is floating or not; you'll need to click the "Data" button to make this variable. It doesn't matter whether this variable is for this sprite or for all sprites. Remember to click the color box in the touching color block and then click your platform color on the stage.

Click the green flag to start your program. Now drag the cat sprite on the Stage to somewhere high up on the screen. It should fall through the air until it lands on a red platform. The program uses the forever block to keep checking whether the sprite is on firm ground or floating, using our check footing block. If the answer, stored in "am I floating," is yes, it moves the sprite down the Stage a little.

To stop the cat from falling through ladders too, add a test for your ladder color to the check footing script.

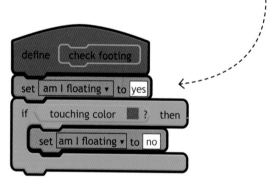

Now add the following script to your cat sprite.

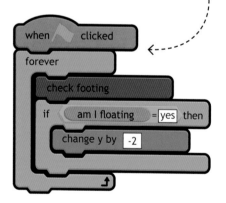

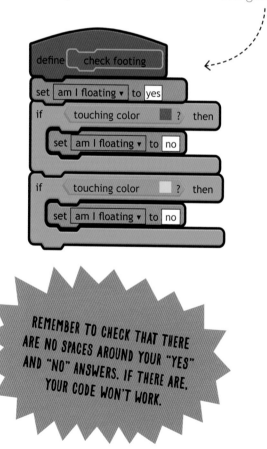

REMEMBER TO CHECK THAT THERE ARE NO SPACES AROUND YOUR "YES" AND "NO" ANSWERS. IF THERE ARE, YOUR CODE WON'T WORK.

## FIXING THE BUG

If you drag the cat around the Stage, you'll soon discover there's a flaw in our logic. If the cat is touching the red platform, it doesn't fall, even if it's not touching it with its feet. For example, you can put the cat's head against the platform, and it'll hover in the air. We only want the platform to stop it from falling if the cat is on top of it.

To fix this, add another color on the bottom of your platform. If the cat's touching this color, it means it's not on top of the platform, so it should keep falling. In the example below, orange has been used because it contrasts nicely with the red. The line is thick so you can see it clearly in this prototype, but it only needs to be a thin line when you make your real game layout.

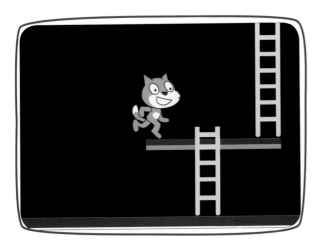

**HANDY TIP!**
To design a new backdrop, click the paintbrush icon in the bottom left, under where it says "New Backdrop." You can then paint it, like a costume. The example shown here is filled with black.

Now you can modify your "Check Footing" script to check whether the cat is touching orange. We put this between the tests for red and yellow. That's because the instructions lower down override the ones higher up, so we put the most important instructions last. Ladders are always safe to stand on, so we put that test last. Orange means "floating" unless the cat's on a ladder. Finally, red is safe as long as the cat isn't on orange.

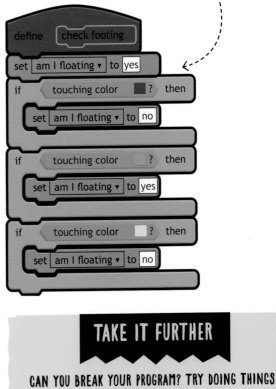

**TAKE IT FURTHER**

CAN YOU BREAK YOUR PROGRAM? TRY DOING THINGS WRONG TO SEE IF YOUR PROGRAM CAN COPE! IT'S A GOOD WAY TO FIND BUGS.

# PROTOTYPING A MOVING PLATFORM

Games often have a moving platform, where the player needs careful timing to jump onto it. For this, we'll use a sprite. We will also need a way to make the cat move with the platform when it is standing on it.

One sprite can't move another sprite, but it can ask that sprite to move itself. The way it does this is by broadcasting a message. Any sprite can respond to the message but, in this case, we only need the cat to respond.

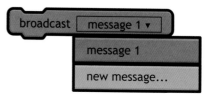

Start by making a platform sprite: it should be red with an orange line underneath, the same as your other platforms. Give it the script below to move it left and right repeatedly.

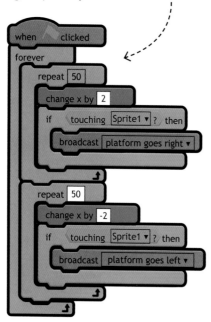

Now, to make the cat respond, you need to give the cat two scripts that move it when it receives one of these messages. Click the menu in the block to choose a message.

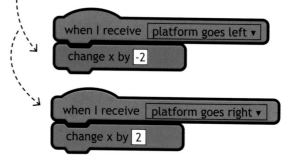

Click the green flag to start the scripts. Drag the cat onto the Stage and drop it onto the platform. Then move with it, left and right.

If the sprite is touching the cat sprite (Sprite1), it broadcasts a message to tell the cat which way it should move. The broadcast blocks are Events blocks, and you click the message menu in them to create new messages, which we'll call "platform goes left" and "platform goes right."

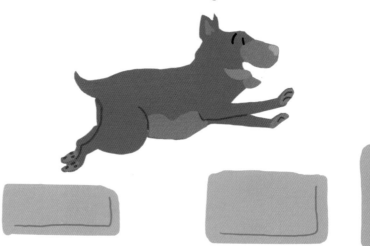

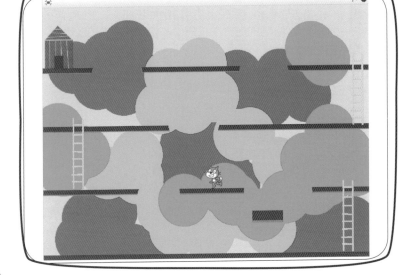

## HANDY TIP!

Keep track of all the blocks inside each other on the platform script. If you get blocks inside the wrong yellow brackets, they won't work properly.

## MAKING YOUR FINAL GAME LAYOUT

Now that you've prototyped the game's gravity, it's time to design your real game. To enable a more interesting game layout, with plenty of platforms to jump between, the example game has four rows of platforms and a smaller cat.

Start by creating a new costume for your level design sprite, and then drawing lines across the full width of the Stage. Then use the eraser to make gaps and draw in some ladders. Make sure your ladders extend above the height of the platforms, otherwise the cat won't be able to climb down.

Put your tree house or other goal near the top of the screen, and design a challenging path for the cat to climb and jump around to reach it.

You can add a backdrop too, either from the library or by drawing your own. The backdrop shown here has some green blotches drawn in to resemble tree tops. Be careful not to use any of your game colors (red, orange, yellow, and brown) in your backdrop.

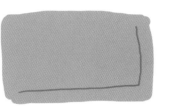

# BUILDING YOUR PLATFORM GAME

Now you are ready to make your game! You'll draw on the skills you've built up from the rest of this book as you add enemies and player controls to your prototype game.

## THE GAME SO FAR

Following your prototyping work in the last chapter, you should have the `check footing` block defined on your player sprite, a floating platform (and scripts to make the cat move with it), and a level design. You should delete your existing green flag script.

## SETTING UP THE PLAYER SPRITE

When the player clicks the green flag to start the game, the first thing we need to do is set up the player's sprite. That means setting its size, position, rotation style, and direction. The `go to front` block can be used to make sure the cat always appears in front of the platforms and enemies and doesn't disappear behind them.

We'll use the variable energy to keep track of the player's energy level. It goes down when the player touches the enemy sprites, and the game ends when it reaches zero.

We can make the game more fun by timing how long players take, so they can try to finish faster each time. At the start of the game, we'll reset Scratch's built-in timer (a Sensing block). At the end, we'll check how long it took.

Add this script to your player sprite to start with. You might need to adjust the sprite size and starting position, depending on your game design.

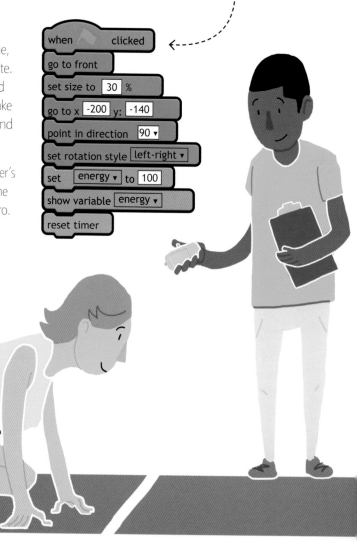

```
when       clicked
go to front
set size to 30 %
go to x -200 y: -140
point in direction 90 ▾
set rotation style left-right ▾
set energy ▾ to 100
show variable energy ▾
reset timer
```

### HANDY TIP!
Remember to set up the energy variable in the "Data" part of the Blocks Palette first.

# ADDING THE PLAYER CONTROLS

The main game loop repeats until the player touches the goal; it includes the player controls and a check to see if the energy has run out. Add it onto your existing player script, underneath the `reset timer` block.

```
show variable  energy ▼
reset timer
repeat until  touching color ⬜ ?
    check footing
    if  am I floating  = no  and  key left arrow ▼ pressed?  then
        change x by  -10
        point in direction  -90 ▼
        next costume
    if  am I floating  = no  and  key right arrow ▼ pressed?  then
        change x by  10
        point in direction  90 ▼
        next costume
    if  am I floating  = no  and  key space ▼ pressed?  then
        jump
    if  touching color ⬜ ?  and  key up arrow ▼ pressed?  then
        change y by  2
        next costume
    if  touching color ⬜ ?  and  key down arrow ▼ pressed?  then
        change y by  -2
        next costume
    if  am I floating  = yes  then
        change y by  -2
    if  energy  < 1  then
        hide variable  energy ▼
        set rotation style  all around ▼
        point in direction  0 ▼
        say  Game over!  for  2  secs
        stop  all ▼
```

Use the color of your goal here. In this case, it's brown for the tree house.

Moves the player left if they press the left key and they're on a platform or ladder. You don't want them to be able to control the sprite while they're floating in the air.

Moves right.

Use "More Blocks" to create this block. We'll define it later.

Climb up the ladder!

Climb down the ladder!

Gravity. If the sprite is floating, it drops down two steps.

This ends the game if the player's energy drops to 0 or below. The cat lies flat on his back. You could add your own animation here!

**HANDY TIP!**
Remember to look for the colors of the blocks to find them in the Blocks Palette.

## ADDING THE GAME COMPLETION SEQUENCE

Add these blocks to the end of your script. They congratulate the player on finishing the game and tell them their completion time. We use a variable called `final timer` to store their time, because otherwise their time would include the 4 seconds taken to congratulate them!

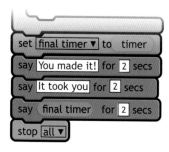

## ADDING THE JUMP CONTROLS

In our main loop, we created a new command called "jump" using "More Blocks," but we haven't defined it yet. Let's define it now.

The jump control is a little bit complicated because we want the player to be able to jump left, right, or straight up in the air when they press the space bar. That means we might be changing the X position as well as the Y position as the sprite jumps. At the start of the jump, we check whether the left or right key is pressed. Use the variable jump direction to remember how much we should change the X position each time we change the Y position.

When falling down from a jump, we need to make sure the sprite doesn't keep falling if it has landed on a platform.

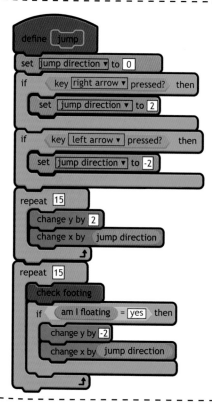

## COMPLETING THE MOVING PLATFORM

You already have prototype code for your moving platform (see the previous chapter). The only thing you need to add is the starting position and a size adjustment if necessary. Insert blocks to set the size and position before your `forever` block. The starting position and size will depend on your game layout.

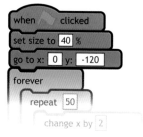

# TESTING THE GAME

Click the green flag button. Now that you have the controls working, you should be able to move your sprite around the platforms (including the moving platform) using the keyboard controls (cursor keys, plus space to jump).

Before the enemies arrive, you have time to perfect your screen layout. You can drag your sprite onto the Stage to reach any platform. Test every jump to make sure it's possible. Ideally, it shouldn't be so easy that you can do it every time, but it also shouldn't be so difficult that players will get frustrated. It's a good idea to make the jumps easy at first and then gradually harder, so that the challenge increases. Also think about where players will land if they miss. It might be quite frustrating if they fall to the very bottom of the screen when they miss the last jump.

**HANDY TIP!**
You can edit the costume of your level sprite to lengthen or shorten platforms to get the difficulty just right.

DRAG THE SPRITE TO THE GOAL TO CHECK THAT THE GAME RECOGNIZES THAT YOU'VE FINISHED IT AND SHOWS THE COMPLETION TIME CORRECTLY.

**HANDY TIP!**
To hide variables on the Stage, untick the box beside them in the Blocks Palette.

# ADDING ENEMIES

Now you can add some energy-zapping enemies in your game for the player to avoid. To do this, we'll use a new technique called "cloning." This enables a sprite to make a copy of itself while a game is running. As a result, you can code just one enemy sprite, but during the game it can clone itself to become several enemies.

All the enemies have different starting positions, each of which is on a platform. We'll use two lists to store the starting X and Y positions. For example, if your first sprite starts at x: 0 and y: 100, your first item in the X start list is 0, and your first item in the Y start list is 100. This code sets up the six sprites in our example game. It goes on the enemy sprite, which is Ladybug2 in this case. You need to create the lists and variable before you can use them.

Remember, you might have more or fewer enemies than in this example and they'll probably need to be in different positions. You will probably need to use trial and error to work out the start positions.

You won't see the sprites appear or move until you add the next script.

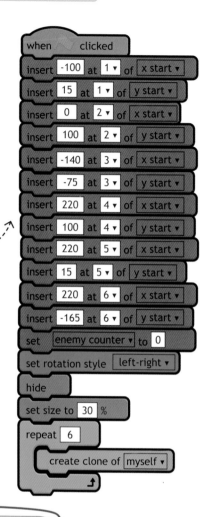

MAKE SURE THAT YOUR ENEMIES ARE SMALL ENOUGH FOR THE PLAYER TO JUMP OVER.

# MAKING THE ENEMIES MOVE

When a clone is created, we run another script. This one keeps count of which enemy number it is, using the enemy counter variable, and uses the lists to go to the right start position. In its loop, it moves if it's still touching red. If not, it changes direction and moves back onto the platform. When it touches the player sprite, it reduces the energy variable by 1.

# FINISHING TOUCHES

Your game is now finished, but you can always improve it. If it's too easy, make the enemies take away more energy when they touch your sprite. If it's too hard, try repositioning the enemies. Try different screen layouts, and maybe add sound effects too.

For a sample code that shows how you can add multiple levels, visit the author's website at:
www.sean.co.uk/books/super-skills-coding/

```
when I start as a clone
change  enemy counter ▾  by  1
go to x:    item  enemy counter  of  x start ▾    y:  item  enemy counter  of  y start ▾
point in direction  -90 ▾
show
go to front
forever
    if  touching color  ▨  ?    then
        move  2  steps
        if on edge, bounce
    else
        point in direction   0  -  direction
        move  4  steps
    if  touching  Sprite 1 ▾  ?   then
        change  energy ▾  by  -1
```

# BUILDING YOUR WEBSITE

Now that you're a game designer, it's time to build a website to share your work with your friends, family, and the rest of the world. In this chapter, you'll learn how to start building your first website using HTML, the language of the web.

## INTRODUCING HTML

Every website you've ever seen has been built using the same language, and you're about to take your first steps in learning it. It's called HTML, short for Hypertext Markup Language, and it is used to tell the computer how the information on your web page is organized. It tells it where to find the pictures, which parts of the text are headings, and where the links should go.

HTML is based on short text codes called tags. It uses pointed brackets, which you probably know as the "greater than" and "less than" signs. Here's a snippet of HTML:

```
<h1>This is my first website!</h1>
<p>It's going to be amazing!</p>
```

You can try this now. Open any program that can create text files, such as Notepad on a Windows PC or TextEdit on a Mac. Just type these lines of code in and save the file as "index.html." Find the file on your computer and double-click it to open it in a web browser, such as Google Chrome, Internet Explorer, or Safari. You should see your web page, with the first line shown in big, bold text, and the next line in smaller text.

> **HANDY TIP!**
> You can experiment with other headings too; they run from <h1> for the most important heading, down to <h6> for the least important. It's probably best not to go below <h3>, though!

**MAKE SURE YOU SAVE YOUR FILE AS PLAIN TEXT. PROGRAMS LIKE WORD OFTEN INCLUDE LOTS OF HIDDEN CODES THAT EXPLAIN WHAT THE DOCUMENT SHOULD LOOK LIKE, BUT THAT WON'T WORK IN A WEB BROWSER.**

## TROUBLESHOOTING

If you can't get your HTML code to look right when you open it in a web browser, the problem might be that the code is saved as rich text instead of plain text. This is sometimes a problem if you use TextEdit on a Mac computer. Click the Format menu in TextEdit, and then click on "Make Plain Text." Make sure when you save your file, you use ".html" at the end of the file name. When prompted, click the button to confirm you want to use ".html." That should do the trick!

# HOW HTML WORKS

The browser uses the tags in your code to understand how your text is structured. The ‹h1› tag starts a heading (or title), and the ‹/h1› tag marks the end of it. Once the browser works out which part is the heading, it displays it bigger. The ‹p› tag marks the start of a paragraph, and the ‹/p› tag marks the end of it. Try adding more paragraphs to your page.

Lots of tags in HTML work like this, with opening and closing tags around your text, much like speech marks. For example, you can use ‹em› to emphasise content (usually with italics):

‹p›I ‹em›really‹/em› love Minecraft!‹/p›

Or ‹strong› for particularly important content, which is usually shown with bold text:

‹p›‹strong›Please tell me if you find any broken links!‹/strong›‹/p›

HTML tags tell the browser which parts of text are headings, important, or emphasized, but they don't tell the browser what they should look like. You could make the text appear in red when it's marked up with ‹strong›, or make your emphasized text appear in a different font instead of italics.

# ADDING LISTS

You can use HTML to add a list to your web page, with bullet points or numbers for each list item. This makes the web page easy to read and can be a great way to organize information such as links.

## HOW TO CODE A LIST

To create a list in HTML, wrap the whole list in tags that mark the start and end of it, and then use tags around each list item. Here's how to make a bulleted list:

‹p›These are some of my favorite websites:
‹ul›
‹li›Scratch‹/li›
‹li›NASA Kids' Club‹/li›
‹li›Minecraft Wiki‹/li›
‹/ul›

As you can see, we can put some tags inside other tags. The list items are all between the ‹ul› and ‹/ul› tags, which mark the start and end of the list.

Add this code to your web page and click the browser's refresh button to reload it and you'll see a bulleted list. If you want a numbered list instead, use the ‹ol› and ‹/ol› tags instead of the ‹ul› and ‹/ul› tags.

If you want to create a chart of the top five heaviest birds, for example, you could do it like this:

‹p›These are the five heaviest living birds:
‹ol›
‹li›Common ostrich‹/li›
‹li›Somali ostrich‹/li›
‹li›Southern cassowary‹/li›
‹li›Northern cassowary‹/li›
‹li›Emu‹/li›
‹/ol›

When you open the web page, you'll see that the list is automatically numbered from top to bottom. What happens to the numbers if you insert something else? Try it!

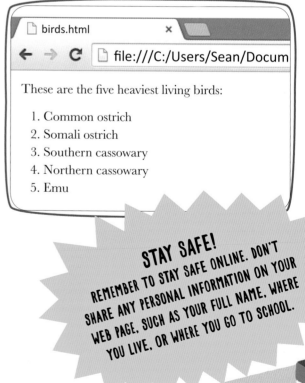

These are some of my favorite websites:

- Scratch
- NASA Kids' Club
- Minecraft Wiki

**HANDY TIP!**
‹ol› is short for ordered list, and ‹ul› is short for unordered list.

birds.html ×

file:///C:/Users/Sean/Docum

These are the five heaviest living birds:

1. Common ostrich
2. Somali ostrich
3. Southern cassowary
4. Northern cassowary
5. Emu

**STAY SAFE!**
REMEMBER TO STAY SAFE ONLINE. DON'T SHARE ANY PERSONAL INFORMATION ON YOUR WEB PAGE, SUCH AS YOUR FULL NAME, WHERE YOU LIVE, OR WHERE YOU GO TO SCHOOL.

## ADDING LINKS

Wouldn't it be great if we could turn those website names into links to those websites? Here's how we do that, using what's known as the "anchor" tag:

‹a href="http://scratch.mit.edu"›Scratch‹/a›

This tag's a little more complicated, because there's some extra information inside the pointy brackets. The first part tells the browser this is the start of a link, and the second part is the website address it should link to, which goes in quotation marks:

‹a href="http://scratch.mit.edu"›

You might remember that "http://scratch.mit.edu" is what you type into your browser to visit the Scratch website. The ‹/a› part tells the browser that this is the end of the link, so it knows it should turn the word "Scratch" between the opening and closing anchor tags into the link text. Try it and see!

If you make another web page of your own (for example, a web page with a file name "hobbies.html") and want to add a link to it, just link to its file name, like this:

‹a href="hobbies.html"›See my hobbies‹/a›

Make sure your file is in the same folder on your computer as the web page that you're putting the link in.

### TAKE IT FURTHER

YOU CAN VIEW THE HTML FOR ANY WEB PAGE ON THE INTERNET. IN MANY BROWSERS, YOU CAN RIGHT-CLICK ON A WEB PAGE AND THEN CHOOSE TO VIEW THE PAGE SOURCE. BE NOSY, AND SEE WHAT YOU CAN LEARN!

### HANDY TIP!

You can link to any web page on the Internet. Just copy the address from the bar at the top of your browser. Can you set up the other two links in this list or add some of your own favorite links?

# ADDING IMAGES

**The Internet would be a pretty dull place if there weren't any pictures. Luckily, it's not too tricky to add them to your website using HTML!**

If you've got a picture handy, put it in the same folder as your HTML file, and then link to it using the ‹**img**› tag like this:

‹img src="my_cat.jpg" width="500" height="350" alt="Picture of my cat!"›

There are a lot of additional bits of information (or "attributes") in the ‹**img**› tag. The src (my_cat.jpg in this case) is the file name of the picture you want to put in your web page. The width and height are measured in pixels. You don't have to include these, but the web page will ultimately display more quickly if you do, although you won't notice any difference yet.

The alt attribute provides a description of the image that can be used by software to understand what's in the picture. This is important because blind people can't see the pictures on your website, but they can use software that reads your text and the image descriptions aloud to them. If you provide a good description, nobody misses out.

The ‹**img**› tag doesn't need a closing tag.

IF YOU WANT TO USE SOMEBODY ELSE'S PICTURE ON YOUR WEBSITE, ASK THEM FIRST.

## ADDING YOUR SCRATCH GAME

You can include your Scratch games on your website. Go into your project on the Scratch website, and then click the "Share" button in the top right of the screen. On the project page, click "Embed" to get some code you can copy and paste onto your web page. If you can't find the project page, click your name in the top right corner of the screen, click "My Projects," and then click on your project. You can include several Scratch projects on a web page.

### HANDY TIP!
You don't need very big images for a web page, so resize them first. A picture about 500 pixels wide is usually big enough. Use an art program to resize them or check their width and height.

### HANDY TIP!
You can embed many YouTube videos on your web page too. Click "Share" and then click "Embed" to get the code.

## COMPLETING THE TEMPLATE

You've learned how to make the content for your web page, but there are some other tags you also need to include so that your website works well when it's published online. Here's a template for a complete web page that you can use:

```
<!DOCTYPE html>
<html>
<head>
<title>My web page!</title>
</head>
<body>
Put the HTML for your text and images here!
</body>
</html>
```

The `<head>` part of the document is used for information about the web page, which doesn't appear in the web page itself. The `<title>` tag marks up the title that is used in search engines and in the tab at the top of your web page. The `<body>` part is where you put your text and images.

IN THE NEXT CHAPTER, YOU'LL LEARN HOW TO CHANGE WHAT YOUR WEBSITE LOOKS LIKE, AND THE NEXT STEPS FOR PUBLISHING IT ONLINE.

# STYLING YOUR WEBSITE

Find out how you can add colors, different text styles, and borders to your website using CSS, the language for designing web pages.

## ADDING SOME STYLE

To change what your web page looks like, you will use a language called CSS, short for Cascading Style Sheets. Your CSS code goes in a separate file called a stylesheet, so you need to put a line in your HTML file to tell the browser what it's called. In your HTML file, add a ‹link› instruction between the ‹head› tags, like this:

```
‹head›
‹title›Sean's web page!‹/title›
‹link rel="stylesheet" href="style.css" type="text/css"›
‹/head›
```

Now, create a new text file called "style.css" and save it in the same folder as your HTML file.

REMEMBER TO MAKE SURE YOUR CSS FILE IS SAVED AS PLAIN TEXT. IT WON'T WORK OTHERWISE!

## TAKE IT FURTHER

CAN YOU WORK OUT HOW TO CODE BLACK? HINT: THERE'S NO COLOR IN IT! WHAT OTHER COLORS CAN YOU MIX UP? EXPERIMENT!

## CHANGING THE COLORS

Add your CSS instructions in your new style.css file. There are three parts to a piece of CSS code: you have to say which part of the web page you want to change, which aspect of it you want to change (such as the font or the color), and what you want to change it to. CSS uses curved brackets that look like an archer's bow. Add this code to your CSS file and reload your web page:

```
h1
{
color: black;
background-color: yellow;
}
```

Save your CSS file, and reload your web page in your browser. You should see your ‹h1› heading is now in black text on a yellow background.

Want a darker web page? You can change the background of the whole page to black and the default text color to white by styling the body tag:

```
body
{
color: white;
background-color: black;
}
```

### HANDY TIP!
Think of the shapes of the letters in "HTML" and "CSS" (straight or curved) to remind you which language uses pointed and which uses curved brackets.

# CHOOSING MORE COLORS

You can experiment with different color names, but the browser might not recognize them all. It knows red, green, blue, black, white and several less common colors (such as olive, teal, and fuchsia). You can be more precise, though, by giving it the number of a color instead of a name.

Colors use a numbering system called "hexadecimal." Our usual counting system has ten symbols in it (0 to 9). Hexadecimal has sixteen symbols. When it runs out of numbers, it uses the letters A to F. Here's how you count to thirty in hexadecimal:

0, 1, 2, 3, 4, 5, 6, 7, 8, 9, A, B, C, D, E, F, 10, 11, 12, 13, 14, 15, 16, 17, 18, 19, 1A, 1B, 1C, 1D, 1E.

In our normal counting system, "14" means one ten plus four units. In hexadecimal, "14" means one sixteen plus four units (which is twenty). The biggest two-digit hexadecimal number is FF, which is fifteen times sixteen, plus fifteen units, a total of 255.

To make a color, you pick three numbers for the amount of red, green, and blue you want to use in it, similar to mixing paints. You run your three digits together with a # sign in front, like this:

| Red | Green | Blue | Color number | Color |
|-----|-------|------|--------------|-------|
| FF | 00 | 00 | #FF0000 | Bright red |
| FF | FF | 00 | #FFFF00 | Yellow |
| 00 | 80 | 00 | #008000 | Dark green |
| 80 | 00 | 00 | #800000 | Maroon |
| FF | FF | FF | #FFFFFF | White |

## HANDY TIP!

If your attempts to change the color or style of your website don't work, check the colons (:) and semi-colons (;)!

## ADDING BORDERS

You can put a border around part of your web page, which looks particularly good on headings or images. You can change the thickness (or width) of the border, its color, and its style. Here's some sample CSS to try out:

```
h1
{
border-width: 4px;
border-color: #C0C0C0;
border-style: double;
color: black;
background-color: yellow;
}
```

The text color and background color instructions have been left in so you can see how they all go together.

The border color is silver and uses the hexadecimal system you just learned about. The border width is measured in pixels (the smallest dot on the screen). You can try bigger numbers to see how they look. There are eight border styles to choose from: solid, dotted, dashed, double, groove, ridge, inset, and outset. Try them out!

- - - - - - - - - - - - - - - - - - - - - - - - - - - - - - - - - - - - - - - - - -

## CHANGING THE FONTS

You can change the font that's used to display your web page. You can't be sure which fonts the visitor has on their computer, so web designers usually specify a list of fonts they like. The browser will use the first one in the list it finds.

Designers can also specify a Sans-serif or Serif text style. Sans-serif letters are smoother, and don't have ticks on the end of the letters.

**Serif text**

abcdefghijklmnopqrstuvwxyz

**Sans-serif text**

abcdefghijklmnopqrstuvwxyz

Some good fonts to try are Arial, Verdana, Times New Roman, and Georgia, which are available on both Windows and Macs. There are many more fonts on both computers. On Windows, others include Calibri, Courier New, Impact, Tahoma, Segoe UI, and Garamond. Mac also has Geneva, Helvetica, Lucida Grande, Monaco, Courier, and Baskerville, among others.

Here's how you change the font for the paragraphs, by styling the ‹p› tags:

```
p
{
font-family: Geneva, Calibri, sans-serif;
font-size: 1.5em;
}
```

The text size is measured relative to what it was going to be anyway, so 1.5 means make it 1.5 times as big as it was going to be. You can try larger or smaller numbers here.

## CHANGING THE TEXT STYLE

There are some other tricks you can use for formatting your text. If you want to make text italic, you can use:

font-style: italic;

To make text bold, use:

font-weight: bold;

So if you want your h2 headings to be bold and italic, you'd use:

h2
{
font-style: italic;
font-weight: bold;
}

That's pretty ugly, though! If you didn't want your text formatted as ‹strong› to be bold, but wanted it to be red instead, you'd use:

strong
{
font-weight: normal;
color: #FF0000;
}

## CHANGING THE LIST STYLE

You can even change the symbol used beside the bullets in your list to be a circle or square, instead of a disc (which it usually is):

ul
{
list-style-type: circle;
}

# FINISHING YOUR CSS

Here's the CSS file made for the example website, using all the styling ideas from pages 56 to 59. You can see the color and font of the links has changed (by styling the <a> tag), and a border has been put around the <iframe> tag which surrounds the Scratch game. If you can't get your styles to work, make sure you're using the brackets correctly and have your colons and semi-colons in the right place.

```
body
{
color: white;
background-color: black;
}
h1
{
border-width: 4px;
border-color: #C0C0C0;
border-style: double;
color: black;
background-color: yellow;
font-family: Verdana, sans-serif;
}
p
{
```

```
color: #CCFF66;
font-family: Geneva, Calibri, sans-serif;
font-size:1.5em;
}
a
{
color: #FF6600;
font-family: Tahoma, sans-serif;
}
ul
{
list-style-type: circle;
}
strong
{
```

```
font-weight: normal;
color: #FF0000;
}
iframe
{
border-width: 8px;
border-color: #C0C0C0;
border-style: outset;
}
```

**This is my first website!**

I will use it to share some of my favorite things with you.

Please let me know about broken links!

These are some of my favorite websites:

- Scratch
- NASA Kids' Club
- Minecraft Wiki

This is my favorite scratch game I made:

## HANDY TIP!

You can use the same CSS file for all your web pages, so if you want to change your colors on all your web pages later, you only have to change one CSS file.

# PUBLISHING YOUR WEBSITE

Your website is only stored on your computer at the moment, so it can't be seen by anybody over the Internet. You can give a copy to friends on a USB key so they can try it out, though.

When you're ready to publish your website on the Internet for everyone to see, you need to find a company to host the website. That means they keep a copy of it on their computers, and whenever anyone wants to view a page, they send them the files they need over the Internet.

You usually copy your files to the hosting company's computer using something called "file transfer protocol," and there are special FTP programs you can use to make this easier. The company will give you a username and password and a website address that you can give to friends so they can see your website.

When your website is ready to go live, ask an adult for help with setting up the hosting. There are lots of companies that provide hosting, and you can find links to them on page 62. They'll also set up a domain name for you, which is what people will type into their browsers to reach your website.

If your friends have websites, add a link to their sites and ask them to link back. That way, your visitors can move between your sites easily.

**CONGRATULATIONS!** YOU'VE NOW LEARNED ALL THE SUPER SKILLS TO CODE A GAME AND SHOW IT OFF ON YOUR VERY OWN WEBSITE! WHAT ARE YOU GOING TO CODE NEXT?

**STAY SAFE!** NEVER PUT PERSONAL INFORMATION SUCH AS YOUR LAST NAME, YOUR ADDRESS, OR SCHOOL ON YOUR WEBSITE OR ANYWHERE ELSE ONLINE.

# USEFUL LINKS

Congratulations! You've now mastered 10 Super Skills that make you a coder. Here are some resources you can use to learn more and build other great projects.

### THE AUTHOR'S WEBSITE

www.sean.co.uk/books/super-skills-coding
Download the example code from this book, plus 10-block Scratch programs you can adapt, articles about Scratch, and resources to help you build your website.

### SCRATCH WIKI

wiki.scratch.mit.edu/wiki/Scratch_Wiki
Lots of useful examples and instructions for using Scratch blocks.

### CODE.ORG

code.org/learn
Find coding exercises here that use a Scratch-like language, including some with popular movie and television themes.

### CODE CLUB

codeclubworld.org

Code Club offers resources to help computer clubs learn programming. You can download Scratch and web design projects to try yourself.

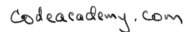

### SHAUN'S GAME ACADEMY

shaunsgameacademy.co.uk/learn.php
Scratch tutorials from the makers of *Shaun the Sheep*, including sprites you can use in your games.

### SCRATCHJR

www.scratchjr.org
Discover the simplified iPad version of Scratch, so your younger brothers and sisters can learn to program too!

### HTML VALIDATOR

validator.w3.org/

### CSS VALIDATOR

jigsaw.w3.org/css-validator/
If your website isn't working, try these tools that check your code. Their answers can be a bit complicated, but they can help point out common errors such as missing brackets.

### WEBSITE HOSTING COMPANIES

www.godaddy.com
www.dreamhost.com
www.bluehost.com
These are just a few of the many companies that provide website hosting services. If you know anyone who has their own website, ask them which company they would recommend.

# GLOSSARY

**BLOCK** A chunk of Scratch code. You join together the blocks like jigsaw pieces to make your scripts.

**BLOCKS PALETTE** In Scratch, the area in the middle of the screen that shows all the instructions you can use.

**BUG** An error in a program. Sometimes bugs stop the program from working altogether. Sometimes they just make it behave strangely.

**CODING** Writing code for a computer, such as programs or marked-up web pages.

**CSS** The computer language used for the design of web pages, such as the colors and borders.

**FTP** File Transfer Protocol: how websites are published on the Internet.

**GRAPHICS** Images on a computer screen are often called "graphics." Usually refers to illustrations and computer generated images, rather than photos.

**HEXADECIMAL** A counting system often used in coding, which uses the numbers 0 to 9 and the letters A to F. In HTML, it's used for the color numbers.

**HTML** The computer language used for the content of web pages, such as the text and images.

**LIST** In Scratch, a way to store lots of numbers or pieces of text in a program. In HTML, a way to make a bulleted or numbered list.

**LOOP** A part of a program that repeats, either a set number of times or forever.

**PEN** A feature in Scratch that enables a sprite to draw a line as it moves around the Stage.

**PLATFORM GAME** A game where the player's character jumps around platforms to reach the goal, usually avoiding enemies on the way.

**PROGRAM** A set of instructions for a computer or other device. A program might be for a game or for a word processor, for example.

**PROGRAMMING** Writing programs for a computer.

**PROTOTYPE** A cut-down version of a program made to test how something might work, such as how the gravity might work, or how the enemies might move.

**SCRATCH** A free and friendly programming language that makes it easy to make games and animations.

**SCRIPT** A group of Scratch commands that are joined together.

**SPRITE** A picture in Scratch, which you can add instructions to. Sprites are often characters or obstacles in games.

**STAGE** When you run your Scratch program, you see it working on the Stage.

**TAG** In HTML, a tag is a piece of code that tells the browser about the structure of part of a web page.

**VARIABLE** A way to store a piece of text or a number.

**WEB PAGE** A page of information downloaded over the Internet, which can include text and pictures.

**WEBSITE** A collection of web pages that are in the same place on the Internet. They're usually all owned by the same person.

**X COORDINATE** The horizontal position on the screen.

**Y COORDINATE** The vertical position on the screen.

# INDEX

CODE